# Contents

# Introduction

**Finch** keeping is a very popular hobby in many countries of the world because of the birds' bright colours, their lively behaviour, and their pleasant song. They are relatively cheap to purchase, easy to keep, and most species are hardy and quite resistant to disease.

Despite this, like any species of animal that is kept as a pet, it is essential to think carefully about their specific requirements before you purchase them, and to understand how best to keep them. Birds that are kept properly will not only be much healthier, they will also be happier. If you are looking for a basic guide on how to keep finches properly in a domestic environment, then this is the book for you.

*Finches are small, perching songbirds which eat seed.*

## Understanding Finches

The term finch, when used to describe domesticated birds, can refer to a wide range of species of small, perching songbirds which eat seed. The canary could also be considered to fall within this classification, but there are now over 40 species of canary that have been bred in captivity, and so canaries are generally thought of as a separate, domesticated species of bird, and we shall not be dealing with them in this book.

**DID YOU KNOW?**

More members of the finch family are kept as pets than any other group of birds. Although more households keep psittacines (members of the parrot family such as the budgerigar), those that keep finches, on average, keep many more of them.

**Small** finches can be found in the wild across many parts of the world. Indeed, in Britain, members of the finch family such as the Chaffinch and Bullfinch commonly grace our gardens. Those kept in captivity commonly include the Australian grass finches, the related parrot finches from the Indo-Pacific islands, and the Waxbills from North Africa and other sub-tropical areas.

Although they are a delight to watch, finches will not generally form a close bond with their owner in the same way as members of the parrot family. With patience, the larger finches can be trained so that they will hop on to a finger placed in front of them. However, they are happiest kept in groups, and are therefore ideal for someone with a busy schedule, as they will not pine if they do not get a lot of human companionship.

*Finches are happiest when they are kept in groups.*

# Species Of Finch

*A wide number of species of finch are kept as pets. The following include those that are easiest to obtain and the most suitable as pets.*

## Zebra Finch

This is probably the species most commonly kept in captivity. It is a member of the group known as waxbills because of its bright red beak. It is ideal as a beginner's bird, as it is inexpensive and very hardy.

The zebra finch will readily breed in captivity, preferring a wicker basket or wooden nesting box. The male can be distinguished from the female by orange cheek patches, a brighter red beak, and distinctive zebra-like barring on the breast that gives the breed its name. Several varieties have been bred in captivity, such as those with crests on their head or with yellow beaks.

*The zebra finch is the most commonly kept in captivity*

*Society, or Bengalese finches are very sociable.*

# Society (or Bengalese) Finch

These are very popular birds, particularly in communal aviaries, because they are so sociable with other birds – which perhaps gave the breed its name. They have been bred in Asia over the past 300 years, and no similar bird now exists in the wild.

Society finches will readily breed in captivity, preferring a wicker basket or wooden nest box, but the sexes cannot easily be told apart, so several birds have to be put together to work it out for themselves. Along with the zebra finch, they are probably the most suitable species for beginners.

### DID YOU KNOW?

**The normal life span of a finch is between four and six years, but individuals have been reported living as long as seventeen years.**

## Green & Grey Singing Finches

These are two variations of a type of finch found across Southern Europe and Africa that are particularly popular, not because of their plumage, but because of their beautiful singing voices. The green species is closely related to the domestic canary, and is almost yellow in colour. It is probably the more attractive of the two, but the grey wins hands down when it comes to a singing contest.

Green singers can be sexed once they mature at about four months of age, because the female will develop a ring of dark spots on her throat, whereas the male develops bright yellow spots around the neck.

## Java Sparrow (Rice Bird)

With its distinctive black cap, white cheeks and grey body, this popular bird is slightly larger than the species just mentioned, and can sometimes bully smaller birds. As the name suggests, they originally come from the Indonesian islands of Java and Bali, but have been bred in captivity in China for over 400 years.

*The Java Sparrow can bully smaller birds*

The sexes appear very similar, although the hen's bill is often a paler colour. They will readily pair off and breed in captivity, with a preference for wooden nesting boxes. Colour variations include a pure white bird, and a fawn.

## Gouldian Finch

The brightly coloured plumage of this bird cannot fail to attract attention, with bright red, black, purple, gold, orange and turquoise patches. There are three main varieties, with either red, yellow or black head colouring. Originating in Australia, it is quite a large bird, and has now been bred in several colour mutations.

It is somewhat more expensive than the more common species, and is not as easy to breed, but is an excellent bird for the novice to aspire to once they have gained a bit of experience.

Just prior to nesting, the tip of the cock's bill turns cherry red.

*Gouldian finches have beautiful plumage.*

# Setting Up Home

**Unlike** many of the larger species of bird, most finches are sufficiently small to be kept in a cage without the need to fly about outside it. It is also possible to keep most species in outdoor aviaries, providing there is appropriate indoor shelter. Purchase your cage and have it set up before buying your first birds, so that it is ready for them to settle into as soon as they arrive home.

## The Cage

Cages can be made either of wire-mesh with a plastic base, or of a wooden box construction with a wire-mesh front. The wire-mesh has to be of a suitably fine gauge to prevent the smallest birds from escaping, so those designed for budgerigars are definitely unsuitable.

A cage large enough to breed a pair of finches or to keep a small group of birds together needs to be about 3ft wide, 18ins deep, and a height of

*Make sure the cage you buy is large enough to accommodate a pair of finches.*

about 2ft (100 x 50 x 70cms). It is certainly better to err on the side of getting a cage that is too large rather than too small. The general rule is to allow about three cubic feet for each pair of birds.

## Floor Covering

Sanded paper sheets are probably the most convenient, but many birds will tear them up. Finches seem to enjoy pecking around in bird sand, which also often contains the grit that they need in their crop. Fine grit suitable for finches is also available commercially.

## Siting The Cage

Position the cage away from any heat source such as a radiator, and out of any draughts. Direct sunlight is often enjoyed by the birds, but they may overheat if they are kept in the sun and unable to find shade, so ensure part of the cage is covered for protection. The kitchen is not a good place for a finch cage due to the extreme fluctuations of temperature and fumes that occur when cooking is underway.

## A Flight Cage

The ideal way of keeping ornamental birds such as finches indoors is in a flight cage, which can be constructed from marine ply and plastic coated wire-mesh to fill a corner of a room, or across an alcove. This can then

*An outdoor flight cage*

# Setting Up Home

be decorated with planted shrubs as well as natural branches to provide an attractive feature for the room. The back wall can feature a mural of a forest or other natural scene to enhance the effect. The floor needs to be covered in some waterproof material that can easily be cleaned, such as heavy-duty plastic sheeting.

## Swings And Perches

Finches exercise by flying, and do not 'work out' with toys in the same way as a bird such as a budgie, but a small swing is appreciated. A variety of perches is important, and these should be made of softwood and wide enough so that the bird's feet only wrap about three-quarters of the way around them. Natural branches from a fruit tree are ideal, providing they have not been sprayed with insecticide.

*Finches need a variety of perches.*

## Nest Box

A nest box should be provided even if the finches are not being kept for breeding, as they will often enjoy the security of roosting in the box at night.

*A nesting box is used for roosting at night.*

## Cage Cover

A cage cover will also prevent the birds from being startled if the lights are turned on suddenly at night.

**Make** sure you go to a reputable pet shop that specialises in birds. Alternatively you can go to a breeder who may sell on birds that are unsuitable for showing and breeding, but will make perfect pets. If you go to a pet store, check that all the livestock look healthy, well-maintained, and are not overcrowded. Some shops specialise in the sale of pet birds, and the staff are likely to have a greater knowledge about bird-keeping than a more general store.

It is always preferable to obtain birds that have been home-bred. They will accept captivity better than wild birds, and are less likely to be carrying diseases. The trapping and removal of birds from the wild, followed by transportation over long distances, is very stressful, and can only possibly be justified for the occasional importation of new species or fresh breeding stock by experts. It is also illegal to trap and hold indigenous species of wild bird in captivity.

## How Many?

It is usually best to buy finches in pairs, and with some species there are obvious differences with the plumage that make selecting a male and a female straightforward. With other species this is more difficult, and if you want them to breed, you have to buy enough birds to have a good chance of getting one of each sex.

If you have no plans to breed, don't worry

about sexing the birds, as two males or two females kept together will usually become firm friends.

Watch the birds in their cage quietly from a distance before making your choice. Avoid the bird that sits, with its feathers fluffed up, asleep on its perch when the others are all jumping around. Healthy birds usually sleep with just one foot grasping the perch, so be on guard if a bird is having to use both to keep its grip, particularly if its head is drooped forwards.

## Introducing A New Bird

If you already have some birds in a group, always try to keep any newcomers in isolation for at least two weeks before introducing them. Even a bird that seems perfectly healthy could be incubating a disease that may be passed on to the others. Do not let them mix with the others until you are confident that they are not showing any signs of ill health.

13

**The** breed of finch you buy is a matter of personal preference, but, in all cases, you will want to be sure that you are purchasing a healthy bird

## SIGNS OF A HEALTHY BIRD

**Behaviour:**
alert and inquisitive

**Eyes:**
bright

**Plumage:**
sleek and well preened

**Nostrils:**
clean

**Body condition:**
plump

**Vent:**
a single opening common t[o]
the digestive, urinary and
reproductive tracts: no sig[ns]
of congealed droppings or
staining that may indicate
digestive problems.

# Feeding Finches

## Seeds

Finches eat mainly seeds, especially the grasses. There are times of the year when insects and certain vegetation will constitute the bulk of the diet, so birds in captivity should not be fed solely on a seed mixture. An all-seed diet tends to be high in fats and provides an imbalanced source of nutrients.

Commercial seed mixes may contain half a dozen different types of seed, but when fed ad lib, many finches will only pick out their favourites. The effect of this can be

*Feeding at a specially designed feeder.*

*Japanese millet.*

*Canary seed.*

# Feeding Finches

*Mixed finch seed.*

minimised by only feeding each day what the birds are expected to eat, so that they eat the complete mixture. A finch will need about two level teaspoons of seeds per day, but this may need to be varied depending up the size and activity of the birds. If there is more than one finch in the cage, separate dishes should be used for each bird to ensure those birds at the bottom of the "pecking order" get their ration.

## Fruit And Vegetables

Fruits, vegetables and greens should account for about a quarter of the diet. Fruit and vegetables must be washed thoroughly to remove chemicals, and they should be cut into small chunks. They should be offered in a separate dish to the seed mixture.

## Grit

In the wild, a bird would naturally consume grit as it pecks around for its food to aid in the mechanical digestion of seeds and nuts.

Controversy exists over its need in captivity, especially with formulated diets. It is best to provide some fine grit in a separate bowl so that your finches can take some in if they choose.

## Eggs

Finches seem to need and enjoy having small amounts of scrambled egg or store-bought 'Egg Food' as a source of animal protein a couple times weekly.

## Insects

Some people will offer their bird insects occasionally and although good for the finch, this may be rather distasteful for owners.

## Mash

A wide range of crumble or mash diets, designed to provide for different stages of a finch's life, can be purchased, and these are generally an excellent food source.

## Other Types Of Foods

The following are some of the goodies that you can let your birds enjoy in small quantities from time to time:
*apple, apricots, asparagus, banana, cooked chic peas, cooked lentils, brussel sprouts, cabbage, carrot, dandelion leaves, melons, orange, parsnip, peas, spinach, tomato.*

*Grit is an essential aid to digestion.*

*Egg food is always a favourite.*

17

# Feeding Finches

## A Recipe For Finch High-Protein Food

Take a hard-boiled egg and mash the white and the yolk together.
Add one teaspoonful of Brewer's yeast.
Add a pinch of powdered avian vitamin supplement.
Mix well.

This can be put into a feeding bowl and left in the cage for 24 hours, after which time it should be discarded. It is great for giving that extra boost when birds are stressed, such as during moulting or when laying eggs.

## Water

Although most finches don't drink a lot, clean, fresh water should always be available

## Cuttlefish Bone

Provide a cuttlefish bone for the birds to peck at. This will help to keep their beaks in trim and supply a valuable source of calcium.

## Supplements

Healthy birds being fed a varied diet should not need a supplement to their food, but at times of stress, such as moulting or breeding, you could add a balanced vitamin and mineral supplement to a moist food. Finches do enjoy being fed seed that has been soaked in water for a day or two and then rinsed off, and powdered supplements will adhere to this much better than to dry seed.

# Caring For Your Finch

## Cleaning The Cage

Finches need to have their cage cleaned out regularly. The litter or sand sheets on the floor of the cage need to be changed when it becomes soiled. Empty seed husks and uneaten perishable food need to be removed, the dishes cleaned, and the water changed. Once a week the cage needs a more thorough clean, with all furnishings and toys removed and washed, and the bars of the cage wiped over with a damp cloth.

*All the equipment you use will need to be cleaned on a regular basis.*

## Moulting

Finches that are kept indoors tend to undergo a 'soft moult', losing feathers in dribs and drabs rather than heavily once a year. A bowl of water for splashing about is fun, but some finches enjoy being sprayed with an fine atomiser of lukewarm water on a daily basis, especially when moulting.

# Caring For Your Finch

*If your finch has access to a cuttlefish bone, its beak should wear down naturally*

## Beak And Nails

If the perches are of a suitable diameter and the bird has access to a cuttlefish bone, the beak and nails should wear down naturally and never need clipping. Overgrown nails may interfere with the bird's ability to perch properly, and will be obvious if they are twisting out at abnormal angles.

You can clip the nails by holding them up to the light to see the pink quick that runs down the middle of the nail, and leaving about an eighth of an inch above that. If you are a novice bird-keeper, ask someone more experienced to help you.

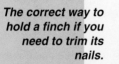

*The correct way to hold a finch if you need to trim its nails.*

Ordinary nail-clippers can be used for the task. If a nail is cut too short it may cause the bird temporary discomfort and bleed for a while, but no lasting damage will result.

# Although finches living outdoors will

tend to breed in the spring and summer, artificial lighting and heating means that those kept indoors may breed at any time of the year. If you are interested in breeding, you will need a nest box, and a stock cage to rear the young once they leave the nest.

## Nest Boxes

There are three types of nest boxes that can be used, and the preference will depend upon the species concerned:

**OPEN PAN:**
A shallow, plastic dish with a felt pad which can be used as a base for a simple nest.

**NEST BASKET:**
A domed wicker structure, with a hole just below the roof for the birds to make their nest inside.

**NEST BOX:**
A wooden box with a hole in one side, just large enough for the adults to enter, and a landing perch just below it. The roof needs to be hinged to aid inspection of the chicks.
Where there are more than one pair of birds, you should have more nest boxes than the number of pairs to avoid fighting.

# Breeding

## Nesting Material

Nesting material in the form of long grass, raffia or even small strips of hessian sacking should be provided. Be careful about using anything with a long thread-like nature, as it can easily wrap around the leg of a bird and damage it.

## A Case History

If you are seriously interested in breeding finches, you will need specialised information depending on the species of finch that you are keeping. To give you some idea of what is involved, we will take a pair of zebra finches as an example – one of the more commonly kept birds that is relatively easy to breed.

The birds should be in tip-top condition when they breed, helped by special high-protein foods that are available, and possibly some live food – if you feel up to bringing home some mealworms! The courtship ritual involves particularly enthusiastic singing by the cock bird, who may well drop a few hints by carrying small twigs and grasses to the hen. Usually the hen will build the nest while the cock brings the material to her.

*Coconut fibre can be used as nesting material.*

## The Chicks

Four or five eggs are generally laid, and the hen will sit on them for about two weeks before they hatch, sometimes assisted by her mate. The exact length of incubation will depend upon the temperature at which they are kept. The chicks will stay in the nest for another couple of weeks before they start to learn to fly, by which time the hen will be thinking about laying her next clutch of eggs.

The chicks should be removed to a separate stock cage once they start to eat seed on their own. Ensure they have perches that are low enough for them to hop on, and scatter some seed in a shallow dish to make it easy for them to get at. Soaked seeds and soft rearing foods will help them to grow quickly.

*The hen will sit on her eggs for about two weeks before they hatch.*

# Breeding

*Baby finches at ten days of age.*

## Identification

If you want to show your finches, or to breed from finches kept in groups, you will need to permanently identify them. This is normally done with special, coloured, metal bands, each engraved with its own number, that can be slipped over the leg when the chicks are between four and seven days of age.

The birds that you purchase may already be banded, and you should check the bands from time to time to ensure they are still moving freely on the leg. If dirt gets trapped in them, they can make the leg inflamed and swollen, and even cut off the blood supply to the foot.

### DID YOU KNOW?

The quail finch acts like a quail, and even looks rather like one. They stay mainly on the floor of an aviary, and enjoy cleaning themselves in a dust bath rather than in water like most other finches.

# Leaving Your Finch

**Finches** should not be left without supervision for more than a day or two. Food needs to be topped up regularly, empty husks cleared away, and the birds must be checked for signs of ill health.

A small cage is easy to transport, so you can always take your finch to a friend to look after. Leave clear, written instructions of your birds' requirements, and details of your vet, if relevant.

## Finches On The Move

You may well need to transport your finch from time to time, at least as far as a veterinary surgery if it is unwell. Some people do take their pet birds on holiday with them, which is fine in a caravan or self-catering accommodation, but they must not be left in excessively hot temperatures for any length of time, or they can suffer from heat stroke.

A water spray can help to keep the bird cool during a particularly hot journey.

*Finches should not be left unattended for more than a couple of days.*

## Signs Of ill Health

- Behaviour – a sick finch will be depressed, disinterested in its surroundings, and go off its food.
- Feathers – become ruffled and untidy if the bird is unwell.
- Body condition – normal plumpness may be lost, and a hollowing of the muscles either side of the breast bone may be felt.
- Vent – a single opening common to the digestive, urinary and reproductive tracts, which may become sore and caked with droppings.
- Eyes – dull or inflamed.
- Breathing – may become laboured, possibly with a discharge from the nostrils.
- Feet – may become swollen, or the finch may only perch on one leg.

## First Aid

Small birds have a very high metabolic rate, so will rapidly use up their fat reserves and become very weak unless disease problems are identified quickly. If you have more than one bird, isolate the sick one, and keep it in a cage somewhere really warm until you can get it to a vet.

Warmth is a very important part of nursing sick finches, as it will increase their resistance to disease considerably. You might want to invest in a small infra-red heat lamp that can be suspended above the cage – but the birds should be able to get out of the light if they feel they are getting too warm. You should aim for a temperature of about 90 degrees Fahrenheit (32C), and gradually reacclimatize the bird to a more normal temperature once it has recovered.

## Administering Medication

Getting medication into a sick finch is not easy. Some antibiotics come in the form of a soluble powder that can be added to the drinking water, but it can be difficult to ensure enough is taken. Medicated seed is an excellent way of administering drugs if the bird is eating. Drops can be given directly into the mouth, but the physical handling necessary to administer the medication can sometimes cause the bird to go into shock and die, particularly if it is already stressed.

*A small cage can be used to transport your finches.*

## Preventing Illness

Treating a bird as small as a finch is a challenging task, and very often the best that can be done is to examine the conditions under which the birds are kept, as a great deal of illness is due to poor husbandry. If you do start to lose birds, arranging for a post mortem examination to be carried out may well help to discover the underlying disease, since tiny birds will die very quickly only showing external signs of starvation once they stop eating, regardless of the cause.

Most veterinary surgeries will happily treat pet birds on an occasional basis, but if you have a difficult problem, you could ask to be referred on to a veterinary surgeon with a specialised interest in avian disease.

# Common Ailments

## Sore Feet

Perches of the wrong diameter can play a part in causing the problem, and obesity will obviously aggravate it by putting more weight on the feet. In this instance, the patient will need to cut down on fattening foods such as millet. Changing the perches and ensuring they are kept scrupulously clean may cure the problem, but sometimes the bird will need antibiotic treatment.

## Egg Binding

Female birds will often lay eggs even in the absence of a mate, although they will obviously be infertile. Removing the eggs will simply encourage her to lay more to replace them, so leaving them for her to try and incubate may be best.

Sometimes an egg may become stuck inside the hen, which will cause her to strain to try and pass it out. It may be visible just inside the cloaca. Extra warmth may relax her enough to allow her to pass the egg. If this does not work, hold the hen very carefully in a towel over some steam, taking great care not to scald her. Then, try dropping a little warmed liquid paraffin into the vent to ease the egg's passage.

Veterinary assistance is sometimes necessary to try and clear the egg, breaking up the egg and removing it piece by piece, or even attempting to remove it surgically.

There is a suggestion that nutritional imbalances may play an important part in causing egg binding – particularly the levels of calcium, vitamin A and vitamin D. If egg binding is a regular problem, check that the diet you are feeding is well balanced.

## Digestive Disorders

If your bird's droppings are very watery, an abnormal colour, or even tinged with blood, this could be due to enteritis, an inflammation of the bowel. A sudden change of diet may bring about the condition, and mild cases may settle down with a change back to plain seed.

More severe diarrhoea may be due to an infection, and sometimes a vet may need to carry out a laboratory examination of the droppings to establish the cause. Antibiotic seed is often given to clear any bacterial infections, and a medicine known as a probiotic can then be added to the drinking water to re-establish the normal, healthy bacteria in the gut.

Parasites such as roundworms and tapeworms may also show up on a faecal examination, and can cause loss of condition and loose droppings. Liquid worming medication is available for birds. Sour crop is a term given to an infection of the sac which is used to store the seed after it has been swallowed, and will cause the bird to keep regurgitating foul-smelling food. A dilute solution (2 per cent) of chlorhexidine antiseptic in the drinking water may clear the problem, but antibiotics from a vet are often needed.

## Respiratory Infections

There are several causes of respiratory infections in pet finches, causing noisy and laboured breathing, often with a bubbly discharge from the nostrils. A minuscule mite that lives in the air sacs is not uncommon. Prompt treatment with appropriate medication by a veterinary surgeon is essential as the condition can often be fatal.

As always, careful nursing, and especially an increase in the environmental temperature, is a vital part of the treatment. A deficiency of vitamin A in the diet can also cause respiratory infections to develop.

## Wounds

Wounds can be caused by fighting between birds, by injuries sustained within the cage or while flying. Flesh wounds can be bathed in a mild antiseptic solution daily until they heal. However, a careful check must be kept for signs of infection, such as an unpleasant smell or discharge, which may indicate antibiotic treatment is needed. Fractures of the wing or foot bones do occur from time to time, and can sometimes be treated with a splint by a vet.